THE POETRY GAMES

VOICES FROM LONDON

Edited By Donna Samworth

First published in Great Britain in 2018 by:

Young Writers
Remus House
Coltsfoot Drive
Peterborough
PE2 9BF
Telephone: 01733 890066
Website: www.youngwriters.co.uk

All Rights Reserved
Book Design by Ashley Janson
© Copyright Contributors 2018
SB ISBN 978-1-78896-483-8
Printed and bound in the UK by BookPrintingUK
Website: www.bookprintinguk.com
YB0361T

FOREWORD

Since 1991 our aim here at Young Writers has been to encourage creativity in children and to inspire a love of the written word. Each competition is tailored to the relevant age group, hopefully giving each student the inspiration and incentive to create their own piece of creative writing, whether it's a poem or a short story. We truly believe that seeing their work in print gives students a sense of achievement and pride.

For our latest competition The Poetry Games, secondary school students were given the challenge to stand up for what they believe in using nothing but the power of the pen. Using poetry as their tool, these aspiring poets were given the opportunity to express their thoughts and feelings on the topics that matter to them through verse.

Whilst skilfully conveying their opinions through poetry, the writers showcased in this collection have simultaneously managed to give poetry a breath of fresh air, brought it to life and made it relevant to them. Using a variety of themes and styles, these featured poets leave a lasting impression of their inner thoughts and feelings, making this anthology a rare insight into the next generation.

CONTENTS

Alexandra Park School

Sam Southwood (11)	1
Emily Daisy Hall (12)	2

Bow School

Maya Pemberton-Johnson (12)	3
Duha Miah (12)	4
Samihat Ahmed (11)	5
Sumaiya Miah (12)	6

Cumberland School

Shade Ogunyamoju (13)	7
T C King Allen (13)	8
Ella Wellingbrooke (12)	11
Sabra Suleiman (12)	12
Ana Sa le (13)	15
Jessica Ezechukwu (12)	16
Mina Durowaa Tijani (12)	18
Hattie Kalamba (12)	20
Aisha Omar (13)	22
Tasmin Esha Chowdhury (13)	24
Tahiya Khan (14)	26
Tricia Nacy Lesaca (13)	28
Anchal Mohanty (12)	30
Diana Zhontsa (12)	31
Keira Ruby Scarfe Trainor (13)	32
Yousef Javid (13)	33
Mamun Arifuzzaman (13)	34
Aslam Ali (12)	35
Zain Ahmed Butt (12)	36
Sabah Leya Mahmood (13)	37
Thanim Islam (13)	38
Fuchsia Fletcher (12)	39

Mustak Ahmed (13)	40
Rusne Samoulyte (12)	41
Samaaha Lecacheur (13)	42
Meena Wahidi (13)	43

Harris Academy St John's Wood

Rawan Janudi (10)	44

Heartlands High School

Nuseyba Hassan Farah (14)	45
Faezah Hasan (14)	46
Layla Carter-Idriss (12)	49
Bryan G Okafor (13)	50
Zachariah Bull (13)	52
Yusra Abubakar (12)	54
Tyrese Van Anderson-Lee (14)	56
Raffi Khashad (11)	58
Gleidis Morina (11)	59
Jeslyn Asare Owusu (13)	60
Zeyna Cekmez (12)	61
Scott Lammas (11)	62
Tamilla Husejnli (11)	64
Linling Guo (11)	65
Sidney McMeekin (14)	66
Ella Macdonald-Boyle (14)	67
Nia Fosu-Edwards (11)	68
Micheal Warecha (11)	69

Henrietta Barnett School

Ritisha Kulkarni	70
Harshitaa Sendhilkumar	72
Vidarshana Sriram	74
Violeta Palekar Fernandez (13)	76

Aditi Vellora (12)	78
Shreya Popat (13)	80
Jennifer Jin (13)	81
Saachi Agarwal (12)	82
Medha Mishra	83
Hana Belete Alene (13)	84
Aliyah Nurmohamed	85
Vedasri Tirumala	86
Hannah Giles	87

Marylebone Boys' School

Krish Patel (12)	88
Conor Waugh (14)	90
Luka M B (14)	91

New River College PRU

Sonny Bannerman (12)	93

Tech City College

Rayaan Abdillahi	94

Walthamstow School For Girls

Amanta Berberi (12)	96
Nihad Sebai (11)	100
Ayjan Jorayeva (14)	102
Amina Asim (14)	104
Noura Athill (11)	106
Ammara Ali (13)	108
Nihad Sebai (11)	110
Sabrina Latif (12)	111
Emily Roberts (14)	112
Maja Mosinska (15)	114
Keira Niamh Summersgill (13)	115
Sadia Arshad Mehmood (12)	116
Iman Nawaz (11)	117
Alisha Naaz Raja (11) & Farah	118
Barakah Abdullah (11)	119
Sadie Allaway (12)	120
Amud Mahad Ahmed (14)	121
Maryam Iqbal (11)	122

Amelia Fernand (12)	123
Aliza Salariya Khan (11)	124
Flora Hammond-Saunders (12)	125
Alba Robinson (12)	126
Husna Lalloo (11)	127

Woodside High School

Hang Tran (12)	128
Temidayo Josephine Ogundamisi (12)	130
Hazel Elizabeth Faulkes (12)	132
Angelika Cseh (13)	134
Victoria Sullivan (12)	135
Aziza Hussain Khan (12)	136
Anastasia Mylona (11)	137
Rojav Alo (12)	138
Ilyas Ali (11)	139
Boglarka Lovas (11)	140
Zilan Eroglu (12)	141
Panayiotis Merkouriadis (12)	142
Amit Tailor (12)	143
Eshan Rasool (11)	144

WAR ZONE

All I need is education
they need their rights and declaration
everyone is equal, everyone is free.
Over there, they don't have liberty
should be in school
that would be cool
don't shoot me down, don't watch me fall.

His parents are gone
at the age of five
with them gone, how can he survive?

Sam Southwood (11)
Alexandra Park School

REPEATING DANCE

Snap - the wind breaks
Leaves spin
Dance...
Shhh
Lights, on, off
and stop
pause
freeze
still
silence
Go!
Yes, no,
shhh...
dance
repeat...

Emily Daisy Hall (12)
Alexandra Park School

PRANKER

As I introduce my dare,
Thoughts I face make me want to race,
Completing this task could be a blast,
If only I could forget the past,
Thinking courageously makes me feel crazy.

When I was nine,
I could finally be the bad guy.
Did you really think I wouldn't get my own back?
Did you really think you would be the baddest pranker?
It's time to play my game!

Daring is my main priority,
I secretly prank you and your property,
As I do many dares inside my world.

I could be the best pranker ever,
But never say never,
Telling my dare poem sometimes makes me cold-hearted,
I'm braver than you when I dare and I'm smarter.

My job is daring,
If you don't believe me come and see me,
It's time to end the game,
Now it's your turn,
To play,
My game.

Maya Pemberton-Johnson (12)
Bow School

FREEDOM

Freedom is important,
More than cleverness, we need kindness,
Greed has poisoned men's souls,
Freedom is what brings us humans together,
You don't need to fight for slavery,
Fight for humanity,
Everyone should be equal.

Why do we need freedom?
Freedom is vital, freedom pumps through our blood,
We must strive to be free, don't despair one another,
We are all humans, why are we so brutal to each other?
You have the love of humanity in your hearts,
Don't barricade the world with hate.

We all have a right to be free,
Learn to love each other,
And fight for liberty,
Let us all unite!
The best way to see freedom is within yourself,
Don't give up, fight for what is right.

Freedom is the key to life.

Duha Miah (12)
Bow School

KINDNESS IS KEY

Walking home down the street,
I grab myself a little treat.
A homeless man begging,
People are legging it.
They don't want to give him anything,
A little something would've helped.
I look at my treat,
I give it to the homeless man on the street.
He starts crying in joy,
I see another boy.
He comes towards the man,
He gives him a can.
It's a drink,
I hear it clink on the floor.
The homeless man says thank you to both of us,
We say, "You're welcome,"
And run for the bus.
I look back at him,
It's getting dimmer.
I remember what Mum once said to me,
"Always be kind," whilst she was holding a locket with a key.
Inside the locket was the word 'Kindness'.

Samihat Ahmed (11)
Bow School

DIFFERENCE

I never thought being different mattered,
Well, I didn't realise 'til Year 5.
I just thought we were all the same,
Only, that's when it happened.
The teasing, the laughing,
And also the pointing.

My own cousins said that I was too dumb,
And I would never be smart enough for a job in life.

Looking back, that is not true,
Because what *you* think, counts,
Not what others think,
So be proud to be different,
Be unique.
Be yourself.

Sumaiya Miah (12)
Bow School

IMAGINE THAT...

Imagine that...
the world was full of love and peace,
and that everyone had gleaming smiles on their faces,
no cries of agony, no arguing,
just laughter every corner you turn.

Imagine that negativity was placed to sleep,
and kindness and positivity were just spread round.

Only if we all accept each other for who we are,
if we all work as one humongous team,
if we are all dauntless and giving each other motivation,
then the world will be a much better place.

Don't just sit there and stare,
you can contribute by giving to the poor,
you can help by picking up litter from the floor,
you can comfort someone in grief,
you can try to eat more fruits and vegetables and start to eat less meat.

Imagine the sky being crystal clear,
no pollution at all,
trees dancing amongst each other as the fresh breeze brushes against them,
birds singing peacefully,
then the world would be a much better place.

Shade Ogunyamoju (13)
Cumberland School

LIFE

Life may seem like a game
But the truth is, it's not about fame
We all go to school
All acting like fools

Woah! It's summer break
Just to make mistakes
Great! Now winter dance
There's always that guy who's a dunce

So it can be said
Netflix and chill whilst in bed
Wake up, go in the bath
Go to the pub, have a laugh

Wedding bells chime
Oh, it's marriage time
One by one, down the aisle
Time by time, ride a mile.

Hospital, hospital, mothers cry out
Whilst fathers worry without a doubt
Screams echo all around
Look, it has been found

Cry, cry, cry in the night
Don't worry, nightmares are just frights

Screams in the garden, full of laughter
When Daddy cooks and he is a father

Cough, cough, cough, time goes on
As the parents grow older
So do their sons
One by one, things numb

We all come dressed in black
Facing facts
Pitter-patter, pitter-patter, water from the sky
As well as from mopey eyes

Shrieks and tears
Give respect, then some fear
Nursing homes now
Hearts are torn

As life goes on
We go with it
Never deny the truth
We all do see them up in Heaven

Life is sort of like a game
Playing cards for fame
Go to places we've never been
At the end of the board, you've won and finished

It's time to put
The pieces down
'Cause as life goes on
We always go with it...

T C King Allen (13)
Cumberland School

THE EMPTY HEART

Dear everyone who laughs and sniggers at that girl walking down the corridor
Do you know how her heart sinks a little more?
Do you know that every day when she gets home, she curls up in a ball and cries from night 'til dawn?
That girl you just make fun of is living an abusive life
She is broken inside
That smile is fake
Those tears are real
That girl you battered in the toilets is thinking of committing suicide
That girl who was just rushed to the hospital for harming herself was doing that because of *you*
That girl who shakes, fearful of the world, strongly doesn't want to live any more
She is empty inside.
Stop bullying!

Ella Wellingbrooke (12)
Cumberland School

RESPECT

What they have done for us
Who they have fought for us
Cooking
Cleaning
Getting money

To me, to you
She's really funny
She stays by your side at night
So you won't even get one fright

The pain of death she has been through
But she has never
Ever left you alone
Abandoned you

They have been through
Pain and death
Anger and love
Regret and happiness

She has lost her life for you
Broke her heart for you
Cried for you
Left her mum for you

Every day, she's crying on the floor
Whilst you are there
Asking for more and more

"What else do you want, my dear? Are you okay?"
She says
While you never ask her
How she is or how she was
Treating her like dirt
Whilst she never
Thinks of you as a squirt

She makes herself wealthy
So you could stay healthy
Her daily routine
Is to get up and clean

Who's higher
In the chart of power?
Is it you?
'Cause no, you're lower

Check on the bottom floor
'Cause that's you
Still asking
For more and more

Oh, my dearest lord
Don't you understand?
Well, let me tell you
About your father

Midnight to midnight, 24/7
Eleven to eleven
Just to earn a little cash
Not a stash

But he works and works
Earning for you
Providing for you
Surviving for you.

Sabra Suleiman (12)
Cumberland School

CONNECT

My friends are my family
My family are my friends
My mum is my buddy
She is such a dear friend
She cares for me
She cares for others
She's such an amazing woman
What a great mother

Thinking of family from far and wide
From lands of mystery, what a great surprise

The way we connect
The love we project
The Earth we share

The secrets we protect
The dark memories we forget
What a beautiful place in my heart
You will always be in

My friends are my family
My family are my friends
What a beautiful family I will never forget
What a beautiful family I will always protect.

Ana Sa le (13)
Cumberland School

WHY?

Why do we kill each other with our words?
Why is it that every time we look in the mirror,
we see 'ugly' instead of 'valuable'?
Why can't people accept the fact that they're unique?
Why are there so many teenagers who put themselves down,
and think everybody else is better than them?
Why do we have this fixed mindset,
that we need to 'talk',
we need to 'act',
we need to '*be*',
like somebody else in order to 'fit in'?
Constantly repeating to yourself,
that you're not 'good enough',
you're not 'smart enough',
you're not 'skinny enough',
when none of these things even matter in life.
Always bothered about people's perceptions of you,
but shouldn't you be worried about,
how you perceive yourself?
Do you perceive yourself as smart,
funny,
kind?
Then you *are* smart enough,
you *are* funny enough,
you *are* kind enough!

Life isn't bad,
life isn't good,
but it's certainly worth living for.

Jessica Ezechukwu (12)
Cumberland School

LIFE

You're in your mum's belly,
Ready to get out,
You see a light,
And hear a shout.

You wake up in the morning,
And your mum says, "Hello, sweetie."
You say, "Mummy, where am I going?"
She says, "You're going to nursery."

"Mum, I want this, I want that,"
This is the stage where you become a spoilt brat,
You never listen to parents or care,
All you care about is your make-up and your hair.

Next is the stage where you become responsible,
Even though it's quite impossible,
Some say it's really horrible,
But, you know, living with your parents is optional.

You've had your wedding and have a gorgeous husband,
You gather your family for a discussion,
Your family asks, "Are you okay? What's happened?"
You get up and get the bun out of the oven.

Finally, the stage where you can't really see,
Plus, you've become old and wrinkly,

You gather your family to say goodbye,
Because, at some point, you know you're going to die.

Mina Durowaa Tijani (12)
Cumberland School

DEAR SCHOOL

The wind swivels
Like a snake
The bell rings
As the birds wake

Teachers' and students' shouting
Echoes in my ear
Such a horrible sound
Anyone could ever hear

A vision of blue uniform
Followed by a learning attitude
Everyone smiling and laughing
In such great moods

Pens to paper
Eyes to the board
The focus is sharp
Like a brand-new sword

The school day goes on
While work is being done
At the end of the day
It will be very fun

Year Sevens, Year Eights
Year Nines and Year Tens

Spend the whole school day
Asking for pens

Never prepared
Never ready
But as we grow up
We must take things steady

School is a place
With opportunities everywhere
Everyone should grab them
Grab them with care

The school day ends
The wind blows away
The birds circle the school
Thinking, *what a beautiful day.*

Hattie Kalamba (12)
Cumberland School

UNTITLED

Trust is a word
a word that is not in my dictionary.
I don't know what it means
probably because I can't feel it.
It is a feeling
I have never felt before
since I suffer from depression
since I suffer from stress.
Every day, a new mark
has been dented on my skin
an object thrown, smashed or aimed directly at me.
Since then, my heart has turned black
with every memory
of me getting abused
of me getting mentally broken.
It's black with hatred and regret.
There are things I will never be able to forget.
My skin is not normal
dry, pale and crusty.
Words are always
targeted at me.
The only thing I 'trust'
is my speech.
When life hits you with rocks
just know it wants you gone.

I wait 'til the day I can make life
fulfull its wish.
That is why
trust is a word
that doesn't belong in my dictionary.

Aisha Omar (13)
Cumberland School

OH, WHY IS IT ME?

Deepening shadows make my bed,
The howling night cries overhead,
Crumbling footsteps nearby,
The footsteps go by,
No attention brought to me,
No concerns nor worries,
Oh, why is it me?

Emptiness fills my soul,
Is there a reason to be living?
Hunger fills the air with no hope,
Shaking, twitching, dark,
Jingling sound comes from my pot,
Never enough to buy a meal,
Oh, why is it me?

Crispy lips make me want,
A warm bowl of cereal,
Will I be the lucky one,
Who receives the silver coins?
It's not much to desire,
Oh, why is it me?

My stomach screams in the wind,
Rattling money in their pockets,
They know they're guilty,
Why don't they help?

I scream and cry,
Knowing I'm going to die,
Neglected as ever,
Oh, why is it me?

Tasmin Esha Chowdhury (13)
Cumberland School

LOST

So lost
I don't know the direction that I'm taking
So lost
The future is bleak in my awakening

My dreams
My life
My journey
My time

The life that I am living
Is it nothing but a lie?

The future is depleting
The life that I'm living
My dreams are fading
Into the bottomless ocean

The life of a teenager
Growing up to be society's pleaser
Not knowing life's wonder
Not living life in colour

A life just in black and white
With a mixture of grey
Filled with confusion
Just surviving to see another day

So lost
I don't know the direction that I'm taking
So lost
That I'm stuck in a world full of misconceptions
So lost
In the life that I'm living.

Tahiya Khan (14)
Cumberland School

MUSIC FLOWS IN IN YOU

A river flows in you.
Except, it's not a river
in me
it's music.

Music flows in you.
Every time I make a chord connect
it fills me with joy
like water filling a cup
like leaves filling the floor on an autumn day.

Music flows in you.
Every time I tune the strings on my guitar
or play a piece on the piano
it creates a feeling in me
that I can't explain.
Unexplainable.
Music flows in you.

Music flows in you
like the serene sea on the beach.
It goes through your body
and into your soul.

Every string on my guitar
and every key on my keyboard
has been played.
Music flows in you.

It's not a river that flows in me
it's the music.

Tricia Nacy Lesaca (13)
Cumberland School

SORRY, FUTURE GENERATION

I look up to the once blue sky
That is now filled with tiny pixels of death
Only a fraction of the priceless sun ray
Takes away my breath.

So used to this life, it doesn't affect me any more
But generation after generation, it gets worse than before
The plastic paper is more precious than life
More precious than the trees that keep us alive.

We talk about human rights
And politics too
What about the factories we built
That are destroying our homes' roofs?

I am sorry, future generations
I am sorry for all we did
Our relation with Mother Earth is ruined
All to protect our greed.

Anchal Mohanty (12)
Cumberland School

TERROR

News flash!
Fifteen died in a shooting.
News flash!
Mass murder in the West End.
News flash!
We are horrible...
Humanity is dead.
No respect.
No kind gestures.
No support.
Just hate, negativity and violence.
Why do we hate?
Why do we hit, fight or kill?
We - yes, we,
We are all responsible in some way.
Even just saying,
"I don't like her hair,"
That's already her day ruined.
We're not perfect, honestly,
But we can try,
We are all one great big family,
So let me leave you with this question,
Would you hurt or harm *your* family?

Diana Zhontsa (12)
Cumberland School

MY PURPLE HEART

Spraying water on a windscreen,
Feeling droplets of despair,
Falling to my doom, I think,
But no, it's all happened before,
Just like when I first found out.

Blood, sweat and tears fall down the stick of my body,
Becoming pale.

Is it a heart attack?
No.
You've got it all wrong.

It's my feelings.
The feeling,
I can't feel when I wake up in a hospital bed,
With tubes coming out of me in every direction.

Senseless, alone, scared,
But all of that changed and became worse.

You may know my story,
But let me ask you,
Do you care?

Keira Ruby Scarfe Trainor (13)
Cumberland School

MY LIFE IS A MAZE

My life has been a maze
Twisting and turning without haste
I've been navigating it at my own pace
For some reason, God has reserved me some space
I can see the world from a different place
I can see the plan
I'm not losing faith
I'm not going to break
I have what it takes to be great
When you emit positivity
Negativity tries to emulate
I've felt the highest highs
And the lowest lows
The sorrows
The woes
But I am strong now that my scars can show
No man, woman or soul
Can ever take my being
You can steal my property
But you will never steal my dreams.

Yousef Javid (13)
Cumberland School

OUR UNIVERSAL HABITAT

I long to see our planet change,
In every chartered country, city.
Towers of nuclear waste, trees of smoke,
The smog sweeps the streets and nature.

There is terror on Earth, danger,
Poverty is striking fast and,
Families are separated,
And have you seen what we emit?
Smoke from vehicles.

We can create restrictions, fines,
We can set ourselves goals and tasks,
We can run and fund charities,
But we have some ladders to climb.

We have the power to change,
We can save our habitat,
Our universal habitat,
We long to see our planet change.

Mamun Arifuzzaman (13)
Cumberland School

THIS UNFAIR WORLD

Terrorist,
Immigrant,
Bomber,
That's what they always call me.
How come a white person,
who crashes into innocent people,
is regarded as just a crazy man?
But when someone Asian does the same act,
he is a terrorist?
Terrorist,
Immigrant,
Bomber,
That's what they always call me.
How come a black person,
who records himself shooting innocent people,
is regarded as just a mental man?
But when someone Asian does the same act,
he is a terrorist?
Terrorist,
Immigrant,
Bomber,
That's what they always call me...

Aslam Ali (12)
Cumberland School

SPACE AND BEYOND

Millions of years ago, it started with a bang
The moon, the stars, the Earth where life began
The sun is a super hot gassy star
But I like dry and rocky Mars
Icy rings of Saturn shine so bright
The moon, the stars light up our night
Venus is cool, but Neptune is cooler
Jupiter is hot, but the sun is hotter
Stars born in clouds are dusty and gassy
Millions of stars make our Milky Way galaxy
Space is amazing, extensive and impulsing
Whilst Pluto isn't extinct, more stars are evolving.

Zain Ahmed Butt (12)
Cumberland School

MY GUARDIAN ANGEL

You are the sun beaming through the grey clouds.
You are the light that gets me through the fog.
You are the car to get me over the rough road.
You are the flower to bloom and look beautiful.
You are the light to guide me through the cave.
You are the star to light my day.
You are an angel in disguise.
You are the night light to guide me through the dark.
You are the guard to guide me to good.
You are the clothes to keep me warm.
This is my guardian angel...
How about yours?

Sabah Leya Mahmood (13)
Cumberland School

WORLD WAR 1

World War One, the war to end all wars,
but another one came in with a roar.

Soldiers, our brothers-in-arms fighting our battles,
while the king is sitting in his castle.

Artillery, firing missiles,
whilst there are children crying like the sounds of whistles.

Ammunition shells dropping to the ground,
while the bullets are piercing through the frowns.

As the blood drips, the poppies bloom,
leaving the excess to engrave the tombs.

Thanim Islam (13)
Cumberland School

IMPORTANT

I thought important things were happy.
I thought there was no such thing as bad importance.
I asked a question:
"Can I see my nan, please, in the hospital?"
Seeing my nan in the hospital with all those wires,
I thought of telling people that I lost my nan,
But worried they would always laugh and find it funny,
But it wasn't.
Seeing my nan in the hospital was life-changing for me,
I never thought something so important could make me so unhappy.

Fuchsia Fletcher (12)
Cumberland School

MANCHESTER UNITED

Old Trafford
Never defeated
Lukaku and Rashford
Get seated

José Mourinho
Always shouting
Once upon a time
He went to go scouting

In the cabinet
Loads of trophies
Will they fail?
Don't worry, kits for sale

Best in the Premier League
Have respect for other sport
Anthony Martial, sometimes caught
Alex Ferguson chewing every game
Putting it beneath his seat
Always the same.

Mustak Ahmed (13)
Cumberland School

IF I COULD...

What do I love?
Netflix,
Money,
Friends and family,
Well, I could go on and on.
But what do I hate?
Rules.
"You're not allowed to do that because you're a girl!"
"You can't wear that!"
Certain rules stop us from being unique,
Expressing ourselves.
If I could...
If I could, I would change certain things in this world:
Sexism,
Racism,
Ageism,
Any type of discrimination...

Rusne Samoulyte (12)
Cumberland School

FANTASY

He walks down the hall with his head down low
Maybe she knows who he is?
Actually, that's a lie.

Swarmed with a hundred thoughts
But ninety-nine are of her
Her face glistens in his eyes
Every day, he cries
Wanting to go up to her
Just to say hi
And be noticed by her eye.

He prays that she will be his
To meet her face with a kiss
And be the one she loves.

However, this is just a fantasy.

Samaaha Lecacheur (13)
Cumberland School

HEALER

The sea as calm as my heartbeat,
Every time we come to meet,
My heart always races faster,
Quicker than the chasing monster,
The one in your dreams,
When you're always in chains,
I need you and you need me,
Because we are each other's healers.

Meena Wahidi (13)
Cumberland School

CHANGING THE WORLD!

Comparing the thorns of roses to humans,
humans are more painful.
You only get hurt by thorns of roses,
when you hold them in the wrong place.
Humans, no matter where you hold them,
you'll keep getting hurt,
just like a gun or a sword.
When they hurt you,
you'll feel the pain forever.
All of them have the strain of changing the world,
none of them have the strain of changing themselves.
It's so easy to change the place of the thorns,
it's not easy to change humans.

Smile;
don't let them see your tears dancing on your cheeks.
Smile;
don't let them feel that they win.
Fold your wounds and keep going.

Rawan Janudi (10)
Harris Academy St John's Wood

LIES

She unlocks the door quietly,
puts down her keys silently,
turns on the stove tiredly,
not having a minute to herself.

They call her a cranky old bat,
not very wise,
uncertain of good habits,
with stunning blue eyes.

They say,
she was once as dashing as the midnight sky,
but now buried with a hundred scarring lies.

Her days are dreadfully dark,
her nights are lonely and long,
every single minute harder than the last one,
depression is one part of her repetitive life,
but as you can tell,
much more is hidden under those scarring lies.

Telling lies to the young is indeed very wrong,
but here's the thing: lies are similar to drugs.
Soon, you'll take one after another after another.

So here's something to keep in mind,
a lie may take care of the present,
but over time, it will eat you alive...

Nuseyba Hassan Farah (14)
Heartlands High School

PURPOSE

Life is what you make of it,
though, that's what people say,
truly, that's all a lie; it's all a fake, beautiful game,
questions always elude your brain,
whether you've succceded in something,
out of all this hurt, happiness and pain.

Your parents pick who you'll love as if it were a dice-rolling game,
they shake the dice, throw the dice and it will just land on him...
He will be your salvation, contemplation and your dedication,
your one-way path to paradise,
that someone who'll bring your desire to achieve something that simply won't suffice,
that someone who'll be your other half 'til death do you part,
that someone who'd be your world,
your sun, ocean, moon, sky,
north, east, west, south,
your lows and your highs,
that special someone that makes your game a little more fun.

Or that special job you were always forced to want,
since you were a kid, you wanted to become an astronaut,
only to become a doctor.

Since day one, you were a robot,
programmed to desire what you do not,
programmed to not think outside the box,
programmed to follow rules, but never envision your own,
and if you ever stepped out of line,
click!
You would just be rebooted,
and arrive back into this condescending world with nothing at all.

Faking your aims and ambitions,
just to make your parents proud of the fact,
that you have always just been second place,
to your sister.

You were lied to as a child, saying that life was good,
only to have found you misunderstood.
Life's a roller-coaster, it's a mess,
there are ups, downs, curves, spins,
until you finally hit rock bottom.
After retirement, what is your role in life?
Is it to be happy that your children can now follow the same fate?

Fall in love, find a job, bring up familes
then it's all over.
There's no replay button to go back to before,
you can only reminisce over the past memories,
how amazing they were,
how they built you to be the person you are today,
realising it wasn't *all* a complete waste.
And now I'm looking back,
thinking,
regretting,
looking at the heartbeat monitor as my heartbeats go
slower and slower,
until...
Wishing I could've had more,
given more,
loved more.

Faezah Hasan (14)
Heartlands High School

WE ARE THE UNIVERSE

We are the universe and you are you,
So don't lose your mind on a tiny error
Because you don't need people to tell you they're amazed or that you're amazing.
I am my family,
I am my mum and dad,
And the blood that runs through my veins.
I am my own culture,
My unique self,
And my own race.
One day, you could be an astronaut,
And the next, a pirate,
You don't need to argue over a minor detail,
Because next week,
It won't even mean anything.
The world didn't make me,
I made the world,
And so can you.
So inspire and be inspired.

Layla Carter-Idriss (12)
Heartlands High School

UNTITLED

Society thinks it's acceptable
All trying to fit in the crowd.
The youth all go out, missing school.
Do they think their parents are proud?
Do you think partying is a must
And complain when you're not allowed?

He said he was about to be the next big star
But I said it didn't look too true
He said, "It's all going well so far,"
He didn't realise the world was cruel.

I knew she didn't even try at all
She got Fs upon Fs and Ds
She didn't know that, when it came to getting a job
She'd have to be begging on her knees.

I tried to get them to listen
I said all the words I could
I tried to get through to them
I really hoped they would.

It wasn't until they were older
When universities looked in their folders
Shook their heads and told 'em
"You're not good enough, all the others have done great stuff."

Never saw it coming
Now she's poor and he's homeless.
Now he's cold and she owns a piece of cloth she calls her bed
Soaking up all the tears of regret that she sheds.

Bryan G Okafor (13)
Heartlands High School

BATTLE OF RACES

I believe in a free world, love and positivity,
not the racism that divides us in hatred and negativity.
We were never raised to be known as black or white,
we were raised to live a normal, healthy life,
not live under a tag the world has given us, it may even be something we despise.
See, see, our colour should never be what defines us,
but in some cases, it is what defines us.
The colour which our skin appears to be,
should never be the reason for the world to divide just by what we see.
The police discriminating against young black men,
to the point that, now, apparently *all* of them are holding drugs,
or committing an offence?
To the point now that Sadiq Khan cannot answer the simple question,
of whether police will stop targeting young black men.
Let's be real,
there's only one race,
nothing's really different but the colour of our face.
You know the saying,
'never judge a book by its cover',
so why do we judge one another?

I believe in a free world, love and positivity,
not the racism that's divided us with hatred and negativity.
I rest my case.

Zachariah Bull (13)
Heartlands High School

THE BULLY

You think you're so special,
The king of the land,
But when someone stands up to you,
You're just a grain of sand.

You don't care about anyone,
You only care about you,
When you're in trouble,
The only person you'll find is you.

You can say anything to me,
Anything at all,
But let me just warn you,
All the words you say to me,
Go straight to my heart and it takes a little fall.

You may think you're cool 'cause you call me names,
And you may think I'm hurting inside,
You may even choose to get nasty,
But do you really think I'm going to hide?

You're not just a bully, but a coward,
Who's jealous of people like me,
Am I really as bad as you make me feel,
Or the person who you want to be?

I know I can talk to my teachers,
My parents, family and friends,
To tell them how you make me feel,
Please let this bullying end.

Yusra Abubakar (12)
Heartlands High School

LONDON

This is London,
Where all types of people unite,
Except those who roam the street,
All day and night.

This is London,
It's a dog-eat-dog world in this city,
Some places look nice,
Some are cold, harsh and gritty.

This is London,
Where some young boys love to carry a knife,
Always ready to go out,
And take someone's life.

This is London,
Where you'll see black and white mums crying,
Why?
Because their sons are out there on the streets, dying.

This is London,
You'll hear police sirens from Croydon to Wood Green,
Blood on the pavement,
It's another crime scene.

This is London,
Tell me, how can this be fair?

We all have big dreams,
But we're living in a nightmare.

Tyrese Van Anderson-Lee (14)
Heartlands High School

I JUST CARRIED ON

They barged through the door one day
Ran up the stairs and took him from his room
Dragged him out of the house
And then he was gone
He disappeared and everyone was worried
What had it got to do with me?
I just carried on playing on my PS4.

The next day, I spotted them again
This time it was an old lady
She started to scream
Everyone saw, but no one did anything to help
They just walked past
Minding their own business
Then they stuffed her down the stomach of a
Jeep
But what did it have to do with me?
I just carried on walking home.

Raffi Khashad (11)
Heartlands High School

DREAMS

When I was young, I had a dream,
A dream that I believed in,
When I started growing up, I didn't feel confident in that dream,
But a wise woman once told me that you can do anything you want to do.
As I got older, I listened to that woman,
And I didn't care what people told me.
I set my mind to my dream and I believed I could do anything I wanted to do.

I can rock climb if I want,
I can write stories if I want,
I can do anything I want,
I have a passion that I am really passionate about,
I can follow it,
Or I can follow the crowd...

Gleidis Morina (11)
Heartlands High School

UNTITLED

Postcodes and gangs
Why don't they just join hands?
Instead, lives slowed down by violence
Covered up by silence

Teach the lessons of responsibility
Or convictions will have you feeling silly
Words hold power
But they may leave you feeling sour

The pen writes the words
The pen where all the power lies
The pen can also write the lies
That escalate to ruining lives

The sword can kill the body
The pen can kill the soul
So which one has the power?
Only choices *you* make will determine that...

Jeslyn Asare Owusu (13)
Heartlands High School

BRIGHT COLOUR ON A BLANK CANVAS

Fat, skinny, short, too tall,
All these comments will eventually fall.
People will bring you down, but you will have to forget and move on,
As most teachers or people will say,
No! You stand up strong and give a daring look to stay,
Wipe those comments out of your way.
Be proud of what you are made of,
Embrace the inner you.
Are you just going to let it happen?
Of course not!
I am happy to be different!
I stand out bright on a blank canvas.
My sayings have made me the bigger person.
I am proud to be me!

Zeyna Cekmez (12)
Heartlands High School

CORRUPTION

Big names.
Big brands.
Lots of fame.
Reaching hands.

Corruption.

Thinking that we
can trust these
lying con artists.

People working day and night
in hot
cramped
painful conditions.

While fat CEOs
laugh
mocking in their chairs
talking business with other
big-headed companies
willing to slave their workers away.

Big names.
Big brands.

Lots of fame.
Reaching hands.

Corruption.

Scott Lammas (11)
Heartlands High School

MY DOGS

I have three dogs
Three dogs I like
And when it's sunny
They're very funny
And in the morning when I wake up
They're always beside me
Waiting for luck
And when it has struck
Time for lunch
They're always ready
Ready to munch
And after that
They chase a cat
Which doesn't like it
After that, we go inside
I let them go
And then they're off
But then they stop
And all I see
Is that they're running
Back to me!

Tamilla Husejnli (11)
Heartlands High School

MY PASSION

I am passionate for reading,
Reading helps me to boost my understanding of words,
Reading helps me to expand my vocabulary,
Reading brings me opportunities for the future,
Reading is *important!*
I like to draw when I'm bored,
I like to send messages and snaps to people,
I like to play games,
Watch movies on my phone.
And I like to talk to my friends in school and out of school because it's fun and interesting.

Linling Guo (11)
Heartlands High School

MY HUSKY

With white and black fur
And piercing blue eyes
This husky's adorable
There's no surprise

Fluffy and cuddly
He loves the snow
Pulling a sledge
You will see his face glow

He is smart and he's clever
There is no tricking him
He found his toy bone
That we hid in the bin

I love my husky
He is my best friend
And I hope this friendship
Will never end.

Sidney McMeekin (14)
Heartlands High School

LIFE

Life is a journey,
Life is a path,
Be kind and you will feel no wrath.

Life is a painting,
Life is an art,
Kindness always comes from the heart.

Life is a search,
Life is a mystery,
Your kind acts will go down in history.

Life is a movement,
Life is a dance,
Kind acts shouldn't be by chance.

So choose your partner well,
For your last dance.

Ella Macdonald-Boyle (14)
Heartlands High School

THE LOSS OF MY CAT POEM

My heart feels like an open sore.
Your life has now ended and
we won't see each other any more.

You had a surgery and never returned
and now I am left
with a mighty big burn.

Even though we are bound tight by love
death will never
become the curtain call.

Instead of ending
it has just become the eternal beginning
that waits for us all.

Nia Fosu-Edwards (11)
Heartlands High School

AQUILA

Aiming high, hunting success,
Merits, merits and more,
Aiming high,
Every day is an opportunity for us.
Oh no! A demerit!
Doesn't matter, we all learn from our mistakes,
In the merit race and the best attendance,
Nearly every week,
Mr Corey, head of house, leads and gives advice and support,
We all help one another,
We are a team called,
Aquila!

Micheal Warecha (11)
Heartlands High School

THAT LITTLE GIRL BELIEVES

At five thirty in the morning
A little girl is born
She opens her eyes
And for the first time, she sees light

She grows up a little
Her teeth start to show
She clutches her teddy in her arms
And believes he is real

Her school starts in a few years
She goes and makes new friends
A happy smile worn on her face
She believes those friends will stay forever

She knows quite a bit now and
At school, she achieves the best
She knows all the Disney princesses
And believes that, one day, she'll be one too

She's so much older now
She knows that Santa doesn't exist
She sits in her room doing her homework while
Believing she'll be Justin Bieber's wife soon

She changes to a new school now
She smothers herself in colours and make-up
Her parents want her to be a doctor
But she believes she can be a model

She's always working these days
She has her tests and so forgets her family and friends
They all know that she will get the best
But she believes that she will come in next

The time has come for her
She's old enough to make her own decisions
She chooses her career and leaves her parents' home
She believes she can earn enough money to buy her own

She's a mother herself now
She has her own Prince Charming
She has her own house
And earns enough to feed her family

She believes she is the luckiest
She has a man who will never stop loving her
A friend who will never leave her side
A job that gives her enough to live and eat
A family who give her all the care and time.

She believes she's in her own fairy tale
That she's a royal princess who can model
She has her friends and family by her side forever
And her teddy bear is real.

Ritisha Kulkarni
Henrietta Barnett School

SHE BELIEVED

Crouched on the corner of the well,
The fairy took a deep sigh,
Drooping over like a bluebell,
For no longer could she fly.

No longer did she believe she could fly.

Her empty back felt strangely light,
But her heavy heart weighed her down.
She was engulfed in the dark night,
For no longer could she leave the ground.

No longer did she believe she could leave the ground.

Her blue eyes turned as grey as the shadows,
Her soft blonde hair turned as hard as stone,
Her radiant face turned pale, losing all its glow,
For no longer did she have wings of her own.

No longer did she believe she had wings of her own.

Into the well below,
Her salty tears trickled down.
They streamed incessantly 'til the well began to overflow,
For no longer could she utter joyful sounds.

No longer did she believe she could utter joyful sounds.

The cool water nudged the fairy,
As it spilled over the sides of the well,
Slowly, she looked at the sun shining so brightly,
For no longer was she lost in a sea of darkness.

Because no longer did she believe she was lost in a sea of darkness.

She saw the baby birds learning to soar,
Showing no sign of defeat nor exhaustion,
Even when their wings and the wind were at war,
No longer was all hope in the world lost.

Because no longer did she believe all the hope in the world was lost.

The fairy gazed at her reflection,
In the well full of tears and grief,
Her eyes gleamed with joy as she saw her treasured possession,
Her wings - she stared in disbelief.

Perched on the corner of the well,
The fairy took a deep sigh,
Beaming like a sunflower, so tall,
For now, she had her wings back - she could fly.

For she believed she could fly.

Harshitaa Sendhilkumar
Henrietta Barnett School

WHAT SHE BELIEVED IN

She was beautiful
though, not for her looks and demeanour
she had a crooked smile
and her hair was dark and lanky
not that which dripped with gold
she didn't have pearly whites
her skin wasn't sun-kissed
she had dark brown eyes
not the colour of the sea
but
she was the epitome of beauty.
You know why?
She was beautiful for the way she saw the world
her smile reflecting genuine joy
which ricocheted to others
the way her eyes would illuminate
luminous in the lurid dark
when speaking of what she loved
for her eyes weren't simply brown
she was ethereal
the way the sun dies for the moon
how waves of silver gently lap on the shore
how the wind waltzes through the air

she was angelic
in the way morning mist
hangs low to the dew-dropped grass
and how waterfalls cascade down
and the break of dawn
the fiery sun emerging
at dusk, too
as the first stars appear
the galaxy standing behind it and above all.
She was beautiful for what she believed in.

Vidarshana Sriram
Henrietta Barnett School

BELIEVING

Believing is a form of coping
Of begging, wishing and of hoping
Hoping is all we can really do
When times get tough, to not feel blue

If only we could truly say
"It is easy to wash the bad away,"
But you forget about those who face their pain
You cannot simply wash away those stains

It is no use praying for someone to fix this
It is no use moving to different places
Unless you truly cannot make a change
In this world of things so scary and strange

But we cannot help, we turn to others
Hoping the world will change for another
Even if it is a selfish act
Happiness is all we need, in fact

It is a wonder why we spend our days
Begging for the end of our dismay
Constantly wishing that time would pass quicker
That school or work could be done with a flicker

We rely on our believing to get us through
We all suffer something, but what can we do?

We believe in things and people too
Wouldn't it be nice if someone believed in you?

Violeta Palekar Fernandez (13)
Henrietta Barnett School

THE LIFE OF A BELIEVER

A believer wakes up,
Brushes, dresses, eats breakfast
And smiles
The believer smiles like
There is no one else in the world
That can smile more than them
Which is true

A non-believer wakes up
Brushes, dresses, eats breakfast
And sighs
The non-believer sighs like
There is no one else in the world
That can sigh more than them
Which is true

The believer looks out the window
To see the beauty in life
The non-believer looks out the window
To see the misery in life

One day, the believer takes
A stroll in the park

Only to meet
The non-believer taking
A storm through the park.

The believer smiles
And the whole world opens up

The non-believer sees
The beauty of nature - the grass, the trees, the leaves
The laughter of children, sweet and innocent
The rhythm of everyday life, fresh and new
And he, too, smiles.

Aditi Vellora (12)
Henrietta Barnett School

BELIEF

Little children smile
As their milk teeth drop
Like stalactites being disturbed by an explorer.
They hide their teeth under their pillows
Believing the tooth fairy will come.

Little children cheer
As they awaken on Christmas morning
Joyful as the family of a loved one who just awoke from a coma.
They run downstairs and open their presents
Believing that Santa has come.

Little children giggle
Searching for eggs on Easter Sunday
Exuberant as a mother who found her long-lost daughter.
Contently, they gobble the chocolate
Believing that the Easter bunny has come.

Young adults cry
Worried about taxes and paying rent
Knowing that these creatures aren't real
Knowing that parents carry out the deeds instead.

Dejected, they mourn the good old days
When they still believed in magic
Because, without belief
There's no reason to look ahead.

Shreya Popat (13)
Henrietta Barnett School

I STOPPED BELIEVING

I believed in people
But in return, I received hate
So I stopped believing in people.
I believed in my dreams
But they came crashing down on me
So I stopped believing in dreams.
I believed in words
But they left invisible scars inside
So I stopped believing in words.
I believed in happiness
But all I experienced was sadness
So I stopped believing in happiness.
I believed in life
But Death whispered constantly in my ear
So I stopped believing in life.
Belief destroyed me
And took another victim
All because I believed.

Jennifer Jin (13)
Henrietta Barnett School

I BELIEVE...

I believe that someday,
I will wake up to a world,
Where lying, bullying and racism,
Cease to exist,
Where we can be who we want,
However we want,
Despite our colour, gender or race.

I believe in a world,
Where we don't have to worry,
About what others think of us.
Where the word 'hate' goes extinct,
And only love is known to us.

I believe that if we come together,
We can bring a huge change,
It won't be easy,
And some might be shy,
But what is the point,
If we don't even try?

Saachi Agarwal (12)
Henrietta Barnett School

SHE BELIEVES NOW

Flying in the night sky
soaring up so high
I saw the wonders of the world
and a little girl.

She was crying on the doorstep
with shattered shards of hope
her home was blown to pieces
and nothing left to show.

I swooped down below
she saw me and said, "Hello,"
I tickled her, she giggled
on her face, a smile wiggled.

We laughed into the night
everything felt just right
she believed now...
and we flew above the clouds.

Medha Mishra
Henrietta Barnett School

ALLOWED TO BELIEVE

Hopeless, lifeless,
Depression, despair,
Blinded by disbelief,
As I no longer cared.

If only I could,
Go back to the day,
Where I was allowed to believe,
When life was merry and gay.

Sunshine and rainbows,
Happiness and friendships,
The good old days,
Of jolly relationships.

If only I could,
Go back to the day,
Where I was allowed to believe,
When life was merry and gay.

Hana Belete Alene (13)
Henrietta Barnett School

I BELIEVE IN YOU

Salty tears cascading like the ocean
You might feel as if you are broken
Any breath might be your last
Look to the future and forget about the past
Stop worrying about the things that used to be
Fill yourself with positivity
You will never walk alone
No matter how old you have grown
If you are ever feeling blue
Always remember: I believe in you.

Aliyah Nurmohamed
Henrietta Barnett School

BELIEVE IN...

Unicorns, aliens and witches too
Fantastical creatures that don't leave clues
You know what?
These things would never exist
So just take a look at your extremely long list
Something to treasure, not only a thing to keep in mind forever
A last hope
A thing that you believe in, even in your last moments
That thought ambles in...

Vedasri Tirumala
Henrietta Barnett School

BELIEF POEM

It can kill
It can save
It can change lives
It can destroy them too
It can lift you up
Or shut you down
Belief is dangerous
But should you stop believing?

Hannah Giles
Henrietta Barnett School

IT AIN'T OVER

The poppies blew lightly in the breeze
As the mesmerising birds flew
The tall trees would just tease

But as they all naturally lived
Hell had come to Earth
The plains curved swiftly
With mouths full of dirt

Raining with blood
And things, god knows what
Boys giving each other a nudge
As well as sharing memories of their homes

The trench, man's greatest fear
The strong metallic scent of pure blood
War had begun

As they acted fierce
And stood for their country
The mud was devouring them
But they stood quivering, lonely, scared

Horror deciding which way to go
Death slyly whispering in their ears
Slowly but surely tickling their spines
Commander Hysmen got ready

The whistle
As if it had more responsibility
And control over them
The last blow.

From then on, everything was a blur
Blood everywhere
Pieces of god knows what on them
Skin? Flesh?

It didn't matter anymore
Memories of their homes flew by
Their kids, their dads
The sweet faces of their wives

They fired their guns idiotically
Hoping it would end soon
Their bayonets lost their balance
Out of bullets

Instant regret.

Krish Patel (12)
Marylebone Boys' School

WINTER'S CURSE

Crystals of snow fall slowly down
Sizzling as they meet the fresh white blanket
That carpets the ground on which I stand

I hear a crunch as my leather boot breaks
The frosty crust - I leave my mark
Humanity's first scar on winter's perfect gift

The lullaby of winter is enchanting
I am spellbound by its silent curse
But I detect a frosty presence

The silent murderer of winter is here
Wielding its crystal blade
That pierces the skin with its icy chill

Dare to run, dare to hide
But snow never covers your tracks
Your footprints will remain

You can never escape the chill
It clings to you; clings to your knife
Let death's icy fingers grip your neck
Stifling a scream as chilling as the cold

The weather outside is frightful
No one can escape winter's curse.

Conor Waugh (14)
Marylebone Boys' School

THE LONG-DRAWN WAR

Down and over
The fields we go
Gazing from left to right
And down, then
At our shuffling feet below
Nervous only of the blight.

Through plains in day
And hills at night
Through marsh, through fray
And mountains with spite
We march on, only bearing these tortures.

When we reach a river
We halt.
When the commanders resume their orders
After surveillance
We proceed.

Whether it's deathly terrain
Or not
We walk as if we have all we need
And like the enemy is still far off
And at bay.

When we hear the general call out
Up we get.
When we hear the commanders shout
We stop once to fret
Then jump to bolt.

These are the proceedings of the long-drawn war.

Luka M B (14)
Marylebone Boys' School

UNTITLED

I, too, am a student
I, too, like to play PS4
I, too, swear a lot
I, too, deserve a life
I, too, hate smoking
I, too, need a family
I, too, want love from people
I, too, want to be a boxer.
Besides,
They'll see how beautiful I am,
And be ashamed.

Sonny Bannerman (12)
New River College PRU

PLEASE

Please,
I put my head down,
I really don't know what to say,
I mean, how many vulnerable children and teens,
Commit suicide every day?
We all carry on with our lives,
Heedless of any bullying that takes place,
From cyber to physical bullying,
Tears to a scarred face.

Broken dreams, broken hearts and a society,
That doesn't seem to care.
How hard is it to show an individual,
That life does not end there?
How hard is it to establish an act of kindness?
I mean, you're sitting in a maths class,
Eliminating the x to solve the value of y,
Let's think of it this way: substitute x into bullying and ask yourselves, "Why?"

Like, why degrade another human being,
When each and every one of us is unique?
Like, why act superior,
Just because they have a disability?
A disability doesn't stop them from succeeding in life,
But you could, if only you'd known!

Everyone has a purpose in life,
Just because they are disabled,
Doesn't mean they can't strive,
To achieve the best and achieve success,
Like when a baby chick is born,
It grows and moves out of the nest.

We have to adapt to changes as we grow,
Like we adapt to the British climate, sun, storm and snow.
We seem to sway our dreams away,
By what society claims is nice,
That the less able 'cannot possibly achieve',
But that's just a frame that creates chains,
And makes it harder to grow.

The trees are inanimate, but they seem to sway side to side,
If that is possible, then I'm sure your talent is locked inside.
Don't ever give up, find what's locked,
Obstacles will most definitely come your way,
So don't be shocked.
You have the power to be great,
Do not underestimate your intellectual finds.
So rise, my fellow friends,
Defeat what comes your way,
Please... please... rise and become better than yesterday.

Rayaan Abdillahi
Tech City College

FREEDOM

Love
Children
Family

Imagine a child, four or
five years of
age.

Walking miles on end
only to find
death
as a liquid
so harmful and
deadly
so sad.

To not drink a single drop
but to pass it on to a baby
a sibling
a loved one.

Imagine a child
seven years old
watching every last
drop of blood being coughed
every last blink
every last breath

watching her parents
die.

Her eyes, dark pools of
sadness
her heart, a black
stone.

Rocking herself to sleep
with the bombs
blasting behind her
a lullaby
a warning.

Miles away from the terror
the loss
the death
children play happily in a
warm
safe
building
storing each work carelessly into their
minds.

Tears pouring down their
faces
not because of
loss or hate
but because of joy

and love and
laughter.

Now, imagine your child
being locked away in a
dark, unforgiving room
every bit of their helpless body
being torn to shreds
just to please
others.

Starving to death
their beaten lungs
sucking in all the
oxygen around them
slowly, surely
deflating.

Their heart being a wormhole of
darkness, destroying
all signs of
hope
all signs of
warmth
all signs of
love.

They are alone
no one can hear their
screams of
agony
no one can hear the
abuse
tearing their little
minds into
shreds of hate
no one can hear anything.

But you
you can hear
me
I'm here before your
eyes
open your ears and
listen.

Freedom
seven letters
one word
life-changing meaning.

Amanta Berberi (12)
Walthamstow School For Girls

AN UNFORGETTABLE PICTURE

I stared at it, blank like before,
No words, no emotion,
Until I saw it all,
Fear, regret and anger, much more,
I needed a way, a warning way,
so then, I began my unforgettable picture...

I stared into the bright blue,
but this wasn't happy or bright at all.
So I dipped my brush in the darkest grey,
because that's how it was: miserable, dark and stray.
I started to think, *where will he sleep tonight?*
But that very thought made me shudder.
Maybe the wall, so damp, so cold,
Or a cardboard box so hard against his back.
So I drew him stray, no place of his own,
No place to call home.

Then a thought hit me like a ball,
What will he eat tonight? No second glance or pity,
But if they toss him a coin, he might've been alright,
But he was always pennies away.
So I drew him scavenging for food in a bin,

That's right, not a shop, nothing pleasant at all,
But do you think he has a choice?

I looked at my picture, not yet right,
Something important was missing,
And then I thought, *there is something he has lost,
And desperately needs.
His handsome smile,
Stretching from ear to ear.*
But it was now worn out and barely moved,
And his gleaming bright eyes, once not worried at all,
Were dark with fear and regret.
His mind deep at thought: where would he sleep?
What would he eat?
Will he ever be happy again?

My picture finished and stuck that way,
Fear, anger and regret!
Could we stop it, could we all?
Because everyone knows,
but no one cares about the unforgettable picture.

Nihad Sebai (11)
Walthamstow School For Girls

A LETTER FROM THE CHILDREN

We 'children' are invisible
Our voices go unheard
Our objections and declarations brushed away with the excuse of
'Too young.'

This is what democracy has come to:
Orange-skinned men high up in their towers
Enforcing rules that encourage hate.
Women and men filing into the ballot station because of those 'pesky foreigners'
Brexit, Trump, both words we hear on a daily basis, words that define
Our future.

This is what hate is:
Riots in the streets for basic rights and silent crimes that
Go unnoticed, unheard
By willingly deaf ears.
Women and girls shouted at in the street
For covering their faces and hair.
People denied the right to identify
Themselves
Even though it should be their choice.
Our choice.

I am no longer a child.
You would not believe what I could tell you about these
'children.'
Where those scars on their wrists came from, how they cry
Where you can't see.
How that girl who sits next to me tells her friends not to
walk home late at night
Not to go near large groups of men because she knows.
She knows.

You see, the fact of the matter is
We are the ones who will pay for your mistakes
(And oh, what mistakes you have made)
We are the ones to inherit this Earth
Once so pure and now riddled with disease and destruction
That your generation has shaped, made.
You thrust this weight upon our shoulders and
Tell us that we do not have a say
In what happens next.

We children are not as young as you think
We know more that you would expect
And yet, we are invisible to you all.

Ayjan Jorayeva (14)
Walthamstow School For Girls

VENOMOUS TONGUES

We abuse their power, using them to mock, embarrass and criticise,
Unable to see the hidden damage, deaf to the silent cries.
Instead of spreading love, peace and happiness,
We use our tongues as swords to defeat any sign of reassurance.

We use them to create scars that have trouble healing because they can't be seen,
We spit them from our poisonous mouths, mutating what they really mean.
They possess the power to heal, yet like savages, we rip them apart,
We use them as ammunition until all that remains is a broken heart.

Like bullets firing from our mouths, we are only content when the target shatters,
Each wound more painful than the last, we aim for where it most matters.
We use them to create such powerful artillery, that no shield can withstand the impact,
Swarming into an open mind, on guard and always ready to attack.

We have been given a powerful gift, yet we choose to use them as our curse
Enveloping the victim in venom, until within our hatred they are immersed.

We cause unbearable amounts of pain, not even regretting for a second,
That in this battle we call life; our words are our most powerful weapon.

Amina Asim (14)
Walthamstow School For Girls

WAR

Everything, all the loveless hate,
The choices that force us to make,
A mess that's so impossible to clear,
Only growing worse throughout the years.

It seems to me that we're falling asleep,
Minds growing distant, we can barely keep,
Our tongues in check,
We say what we think,
When we think,
Even though so many people don't think anymore.

It almost hurts to know it took one word to ignite,
All the wars in the world, I don't like to think it might,
End in defeat and death and all things painful,
There's no such thing in the world as hate that's sustainable.

The idea we need tears to feel happiness,
Is an idea that's just so careless,
A precedent, a leg for destruction to stand on,
Is not needed for us all to live from.

Just put down your weapons,
Keep your views, minus any aggression,
We're free to feel,
But not if it makes someone else feel,

Like they can't reveal,
Their thoughts.

No one should have to hide away,
Save their prayers for another day,
When they're free,
So think about what I said,
And feel free to take it personally.

Noura Athill (11)
Walthamstow School For Girls

A DREAM OF BELIEF

Dreams,
What are they?
Will they come true?
Whether it's above the clouds,
Or under the sea,
Who do you aspire to be?
Famous, intelligent, inventor,
Will you be called by these names?
Or will you be led into heart-sinking pain?
Not if you take the path of belief,
Of God and yourself,
Using the heart and mind,
With determination and pride!
One priceless thing in life is hard work,
Pushing yourself, to the farthest you can be,
Will lead you to your dream,
You'll see!
No competition or race,
Just challenging yourself at a quicker pace,
Do you want your name,
To be tattooed into the world?
The feelings of respect even when you've left,
Just follow the shining beams of light,
Which lead you to your destination, ever so nice!

Life will take its turns,
Like the different chapters in a book,
Look on the bright side,
Be strong, work hard and never give up,
'Til your last,
Always believe in your dream,
And that's how you'll achieve!

Ammara Ali (13)
Walthamstow School For Girls

POLLUTION

Watch the darkness looming everywhere, all of it blurred out,
Stare at the traffic, cars releasing gas, all of this pollution.
And hold your breath in fear and disgust,
Ask yourself, is there a solution?

Look in those lifeless neighbourhoods, a dreadful sight,
The silent screams and crying trees.
The burnt, fallen leaves from all the wicked pollution,
Ask yourself, is there a solution?

Dive into the ocean, be confused by the cramped blue,
Caught up in the never-ending, decaying plastic.
Stare in the eyes, the dying eyes,
Or breathless, innocent animals.
We caused this pollution!
Ask yourself, is there a solution?

There is pollution everywhere, even at your feet,
It lies around, getting bigger every time we sleep.
We can solve it, if we aren't goons,
But if we don't, then we'll have to move to the moon!

Nihad Sebai (11)
Walthamstow School For Girls

BELIEVE IN YOURSELF

Believe in yourself when you have a fear,
But don't fall into tears,
Whatever happens, happens for good,
Don't hide yourself under the hood.

Believe in yourself when it's hard to achieve,
Leave all of your negativity up your sleeve,
Whatever your heart says to you,
That is what you should do.

Believe in yourself when you can't reach your goal,
Because you can go higher than a pole,
Life is not in order like lists,
It's full of many twists.

Believe in yourself when you are alone,
You have the potential to fly like a drone,
Show everyone who you are,
And then you will shine like a star.

Believe in yourself and let yourself free,
Then what can you see,
That gives you glee?
Believe in yourself, as our school gives you belief,
'Neglect not the gift that is in thee'.

Sabrina Latif (12)
Walthamstow School For Girls

THE GIRL WHO MAKES NO SOUND

You might see her around
Behind the shadows, behind the crowds
She'll be lurking in the background
The girl who makes no sound.
Her silent whispers can't be heard
You listen, but not a word
Like a quiet, lonesome bird
The girl who makes no sound.
After hours, she stands right there
A small, petite girl with frailed hair
I turn around and see, out of nowhere
The girl who makes no sound.
Her eyes as red as blood
Her skin as white as chalk
She reaches to touch my hair
And prods her lips, as if to talk
She tries to open her bruised little mouth
But I now know why she's so weak
For I see stitches along her lips
Forbidding her to speak.
Her lips have been sewn together

No reason is found
But now I know why
The girl makes no sound.

Emily Roberts (14)
Walthamstow School For Girls

I MISS YOU

I remember your dimpled, wide smile that would always grow
On my return to our little magical world
Where we would laugh and shop and bake
Happy memories we did make

I remember your bright, ocean eyes
Filled with adventures and surprise
And your amazing warm laugh which would always break
Those hard shells that I would create

I remember the memories that we shared
And no matter what, you always cared
Through thick and thin, you stayed
And put me back when I would stray

Now that time has slipped past
I wish I had a time machine in my grasp
For then I could travel back and relive
Those darkened days relit

I miss you, Grandma...

Maja Mosinska (15)
Walthamstow School For Girls

STOP THE HATE

*'Courage is being yourself
In a world that tells you to be someone else'.*

We're here, we're queer and we wanna shout
In a society that might hurt us if we come out

Some of us are lucky - we can make it every day
Just being ourselves and knowing that's okay

Still, there are others living constantly in fear
If they let on who they are, they'll lose all they hold dear

You've got some privilege, with you being straight
The least we're asking of you is that you don't hate

Because too many people have lost their voice
Being bullied for something that isn't their choice.

Keira Niamh Summersgill (13)
Walthamstow School For Girls

WHY?

Why do we judge a person by their cover?
Why do we question what everyone does?
Why do we accept what society thinks?
Why is there so much hatred in the world?
Why is there so much backbiting on this Earth?
Why do we not achieve anything despite what's happening?
We can't control everything, but we can make a difference.
Why don't you make a difference?
Why don't you change the world?
Why don't you be the better person?
Why don't you be the bigger person?
Why don't you accept other people?
Why don't you make the world a better place?
Change the world and make it a better place.

Sadia Arshad Mehmood (12)
Walthamstow School For Girls

POVERTY

P lease help the unfortunate people in the world - stop and think and give 'em a drink.
O pen your mind and donate to these people with food and drink they cannot find.
V arious people are different from others - some poor, some rich, some fat and thin.
E veryone is different in this world, so don't judge them, it is impolite.
'R eady to get rid of poverty' is this year's resolution.
T ime for us all to erradicate the misfortune of these people, so let's help them out!
Y esterday was full of dismay, but tomorrow is a new day for us all to help in some way, in any way.

Iman Nawaz (11)
Walthamstow School For Girls

BULLYING

Why do people talk about the colour of my skin?
Or whether I'm fat or whether I'm thin?
You call me a loser
You call me a fool
I ain't got a choice on going back to school

You push me around and knock me on the ground
You call me fat and you call me round
You mock me for crying tears
And I think I can't say anything because nobody cares

I start to open up and tell people more
And everyone helps me because of what they saw
I have learnt now not to cry with tears
Because now I know that everyone cares.

Alisha Naaz Raja (11) & Farah
Walthamstow School For Girls

HUMAN RIGHTS

What's this word?
It sounds absurd.
What's this thing?
It's called 'human rights'.

Because we have a right to speak
We have a right to sleep
We have a right to run
We have a right to have fun.

Because we are humans
And nobody is more superior
Than anybody else
Because we are human
So, for Heaven's sake
Don't let anybody hold you down
Because we're human
And, in the end
We need to fight for our rights
Woman or man...
Fight.

Barakah Abdullah (11)
Walthamstow School For Girls

THE UNFORTUNATE

I saw a child begging,
a look of hunger on her face,
she's begging for her mother,
who's in a hard place.

I saw a little boy crying,
praying in the graveyard.
His father died at war,
now he must work hard.

I saw a woman with a black eye,
because her boyfriend abuses her.
All these different things,
they're giving me nausea.

The world isn't fair,
we go without a care,
the wind flowing in our hair.
When the unfortunate see us,
they just stare.

Sadie Allaway (12)
Walthamstow School For Girls

BE NO ONE BUT YOURSELF

I could count a million stars
and still not know
why people hate?
Why people discriminate?
Why the desire to incriminate?
I'm black, you're white
it's our basic human rights
doesn't matter who you are
whether you're Asian, African or socially unknown
There's always a place where you will be embraced
for your difference
For your personality.
No more racist comments
live life the way *you* want.
Be proud
be loud
be no one but yourself.

Amud Mahad Ahmed (14)
Walthamstow School For Girls

DEFORESTATION

Deforestation, the cause of animals
losing their adaptation.
A thing that goes round in rotation
a thing for all humans that is a humiliation.
Some are cut down by companies to build so-called 'foundations'
some are cut down for their cattle's duplication.
Illegal logging occurs from Brazil to Indonesia, a huge violation.
Mining is also a problem and so is the Earth's radiation.
Together, as a nation
we can become an association
and end deforestation!

Maryam Iqbal (11)
Walthamstow School For Girls

A BETTER PLACE

This world can be a better place,
all our happiness is kept in a case,
buried down, out of sight,
so all our spite,
comes into might.

Children are sick and dying,
their parents are crying.
People are starving,
whilst others are laughing.

People are dying,
where there is supposed to be fun,
while some people die,
for just half a bun.

All our happiness is being kept in a case,
this world could be a better place.

Amelia Fernand (12)
Walthamstow School For Girls

GOD

I always believe and never deceive Him.

I call Him Allah,
some call Him Lord,
and some call Him Elohim.
He gave me a home,
he gave me freewill.

When it is dark,
he is my light.
When I am clueless,
he has my answer.

Whatever I do,
wherever I go,
God is my guide,
God is my kind,
and I am His subject.

God is my everything,
I do believe in Him,
I do, I do.

Aliza Salariya Khan (11)
Walthamstow School For Girls

HOPE

Bullying,
Oppression,
Animal rights,
Gender equality,
Global warming,
Racism,
Religious intolerance,
Homophobia,
War,
Corporate greed,
Anti-abortion,
Unfair trade,
Irresponsible food industry,
Psychiatric survivors,
Time's up.
Where should I start?
A small glimpse of hope slides down the face of good,
But can we stop this?
The spread is thick on a thin crust.

Flora Hammond-Saunders (12)
Walthamstow School For Girls

WHY?

Why do we judge people on how they look?
What do you think when you see a girl with a headscarf?
Now, take that headscarf off.
What do you think now?

What do you think when you see
Lighter-coloured skin?
What do you think of when you see
Darker-coloured skin?

Whatever you think
Erase it.
Whenever, wherever, whoever
Smile at everyone
Be grateful.

Alba Robinson (12)
Walthamstow School For Girls

RECYCLING

Scattered along, I see all sorts of bottles, big and small
I stand up tall
And pick them all
Taking them to be recycled.
When I see them go away
I start to say, "Hip hip hooray!"
Because today
I saved the day.
If only everyone recycled, too
Then there wouldn't be as much to do.

Husna Lalloo (11)
Walthamstow School For Girls

ART

Art is my favourite, no question
However, art does not mean literal perfection
You can draw straight lines without any caution
No real meaning - everyone's different interpretation

Don't compare yourself to others, there's no competition
Everyone's style differs (please take that into consideration)
Art can be anything, it doesn't have to be physical presentation
It can be in songs and may even slip into our conversations

Some people don't use words to gain appreciation
A picture tells a thousand words, equal amount of expression
Intended to be acknowledged for their beauty and strong emotion
Art can be moving or bring you great satisfaction

From paintings, buildings and fashion
It's circled around us for many generations
Since we were babies, it has always been our foundation
Art brings us together and builds strong connection

If you want to be an artist, that is a great ambition
But it requires determination, dedication and motivation
Because if your art has been called ugly, that is just an assumption
For everything that we create is a masterpiece, not a humiliation

This is why art is so important, brought into our education
It teaches us to learn from the journey not the destination
No matter what you're doing or your location
What lies in your palms is your very own creation

May this be an introduction
For everyone who is in confusion
For everyone who thinks 'artist' is not a real profession
For everyone who cannot think of a definition
And for everyone who thinks there are no imperfections

Anyone can make art, just use your imagination.

Hang Tran (12)
Woodside High School

HUMANS, NOT COLOURS

I've had enough of being a colour
I am not black or white or anything in-between that
No matter how many pounds, cents or dollars
I will never be labelled just by what is seen
And yes, I am here to holler.

From birth, society force-feeds us tags
Categories
Trademarks
Brands.

But it's all wrong - we need to stop
Who we are isn't skin deep
You can't just buy who you are from your local corner shop
It's what's inside, who you are, your personality
I don't mind your race or gender - those things you cannot swap.

I might only be twelve years old
But before you disregard my plea
I want you to think and see.

Who would you be if you were never labelled?
Are you going to let a fake label define yourself?
Listen to what I'm saying, none of this is a fable.

I'm still in secondary school
But even I know we were meant to be free
No one is a colour
I'm not a colour.
I am me.

Temidayo Josephine Ogundamisi (12)
Woodside High School

M E

My name is Harriet
I'm cool and funny
And people admire me
I've travelled the world
And can speak multiple languages
This is me

Except it's not

My name is Hazel
I may not have the best looks
Or be the coolest kid at school
I may not have travelled the world
And I can only speak English

This is the true me

And I love myself for who I am
No matter what people think of me
I surround myself with people who love me for me
Rather than wanting me to change

Being your own quirky self is way more interesting than being anyone else

So don't believe that
Making yourself look like everyone else
Or pretending to be someone you're not
Will make you stand out

Because it doesn't

If you do your own thing
Rather than everyone else's
That's beautiful
And that's strong

So be yourself
Everyone else is taken.

Hazel Elizabeth Faulkes (12)
Woodside High School

BLINK OF AN EYE

Standing on the edge of the cliff
I stared into her emerald eyes
Her face look expressionless
Like she had no secret to tell
She placed her finger to her mouth
I understood the sign
She was about to leave me
I nodded and accepted her goodbye
She didn't really talk
Only gestured and signed
Stepped back, I closed my eyes
Counting in my head, three numbers
One... two... three...
Instantly, I felt the magic sparks on my face
I lunged back a couple of steps
Opening my eyes, I saw
That in the blink of an eye
My dear Lydia
Was gone.

Now I wait for another hundred years
'Til me and my Lydia
Are reunited once more.

Angelika Cseh (13)
Woodside High School

DILEMMA

I hate your expectations
I really do
I try and try but
That's not good enough for you.
I can work day and night
But I'm still not there
Though I try so hard to be like you want me to.

I can only try my best
And that's all I can do.
I want to be free to daydream
And draw the whole day through
But I can't do that
Since it's not good enough for you.

In the mirror, I see disappointment in your eyes
My dreams have been chased away.
We are so different, but
We are two sides of the same coin.
If we could only be together
If we could balance what we could do
I would surely, then, be good enough for you.

Victoria Sullivan (12)
Woodside High School

WORLD WAR TWO

I think back to the days when it wasn't fair,
Blood and guns were everywhere.
I researched about the war and found out lots,
Those poor soldiers, they must have suffered from a lot of shots.

I can't imagine how it must've felt,
Little children wondering about their fathers silently,
Mothers worried about their sons constantly,
As well as all the soldiers with the thoughts and feelings that just won't melt.

I clench my fists and grit my teeth,
Reading a site about the war, I think very deep,
However, I end up falling into a deep night's sleep.

Aziza Hussain Khan (12)
Woodside High School

FRIENDS

'Friends', is that what you call them?
'Friends', the ones who bully you and shout because they want everything their way.
'Friends', the ones who are kind, but once you know them, they throw you into the dirt.
Is that what you call friendship?
Are they true? I don't think so.
They laugh and giggle at you
but you don't care.
At their birthday, you use all your money.
At your birthday, they don't even turn up.
'Friends', the mean and cruel ones.
'Friends'.
They may be mean, but they are still your friends...

Anastasia Mylona (11)
Woodside High School

I WISH

I wish I could scream
I wish I could be free
I wish I had a chance
to go very, very far

I wish I had confidence
No more hiding in the shadows
I wish I had inspiration
So I could speak out loud
I wish I had an imagination
No more running from the land of fears
My heart broken like a million pieces of glass.

I wish there was world peace
I wish I could vote.

Now I've explained my point
I think it's time to go
To follow the steps
To be on top of the world.

Rojav Alo (12)
Woodside High School

WE ARE STILL HUMAN

I may be black, you may be white.
I may be white, you may be black.
Our actions may not be the same,
but keep in mind, we are still human.

No need for protesting
as that is time-consuming.
More and more people every day are just not realising.
Being racist, where does it get you?
Surely there is something else you could do?
Muslim, Christian, Jewish, whatever your religion,
we're all human.
Can't you get that through your head,
why is that so hard to accept?

Ilyas Ali (11)
Woodside High School

FAMILY

DNA does not define our parents
Blood does not define our brothers, sisters
My fingerprint isn't my father's
My voice doesn't resemble Vicki's
But they are family.

My eyes aren't Emma's
My hair not Hailey's
But they still find a place in my heart
The true definition of love
No marks and no scars
Dig deeper and you'll find
Not in my mind
But in my life
People who care more than anyone by far.

Boglarka Lovas (11)
Woodside High School

LIES

Roses aren't always red
And violets aren't exactly blue
The society that we live in
Doesn't always seem to tell the truth

Smiles aren't always happy
And frowns aren't always sad
Our feelings are what matters,
but people seem to forget

Some words aren't always meant
And life isn't always perfect
Actions speak louder than words
So next time, think, *is it worth it?*

Zilan Eroglu (12)
Woodside High School

POVERTY

Not the lady at Greggs who kneads the bread,
but the lady who begs and needs for bread,
the man who works up in the hills,
or the teenagers in the poverty-stricken areas,
selling drugs from day 'til night,
because their parents can't get jobs.
Not the man who sips champagne on a plane,
but the hundreds of thousands of immigrants,
who die trying to cross seas.

Panayiotis Merkouriadis (12)
Woodside High School

WHY?

Why do I harm myself with words of hate?
Why do I run from the fights that I cause?
Why do I bully?
Why do I cut the bond of friendship?
Why do I lie?

I harm myself with words 'cause I get bullied.
I run 'cause I am scared.
I bully 'cause I want to fit in.
I break the bond so that others don't think I am lame.
I lie to hide my weakness.

Amit Tailor (12)
Woodside High School

I'M A MUSLIM MAN

I am a Muslim, not a terrorist
I'm not the people who go and bomb innocent people
I'm a guy who studies my religion
and nowhere in it does it say to go and bomb people
'cause we are Muslims, not terrorists.
True Muslim people don't bomb
believe me, that is a fact for you.
believe me: I'm not a terrorist
I'm a Muslim man, not a terrorist.

Eshan Rasool (11)
Woodside High School

YOUNG WRITERS INFORMATION

We hope you have enjoyed reading this book – and that you will continue to in the coming years.

If you're a young writer who enjoys reading and creative writing, or the parent of an enthusiastic poet or story writer, do visit our website **www.youngwriters.co.uk**. Here you will find free competitions, workshops and games, as well as recommended reads, a poetry glossary and our blog.

If you would like to order further copies of this book, or any of our other titles, then please give us a call or visit **www.youngwriters.co.uk**.

Young Writers
Remus House
Coltsfoot Drive
Peterborough
PE2 9BF
(01733) 890066
info@youngwriters.co.uk

@YoungWritersUK   @YoungWritersCW